Touches

TOUCHES

Journey to Healing

MARLENE J. DOUGLAS

XULON PRESS

Xulon Press
2301 Lucien Way #415
Maitland, FL 32751
407.339.4217

www.xulonpress.com

Unless otherwise indicated, Scripture quotations taken from the
King James Version (KJV)–*public domain.*

Scripture quotations taken from the Holy Bible, New International
Version (NIV). Copyright © 1973, 1978, 1984, 2011 by Biblica,
Inc.™. Used by permission. All rights reserved.

Printed in the United States of America

Paperback ISBN-13: 978-1-6628-4104-0

Ebook ISBN-13: 978-1-6628-4105-7

Table of Contents

Introduction

*M*y first book, "Touches Who Am I" is based on my life, from birth into adulthood. This book is a continuation of the essence of what I've been through, what I've been doing, my healing process, and how I got there.

While on this journey, I went through a season that tested my faith in God. If it were not for the grace of God, I would not have made it through.

My Process

*M*y book *Touches Who Am I* was published during a time when my marriage was falling to pieces starting in 2018, during which I learned to solely depend on God. I was battling different emotions and I was falling apart, not to mention, the roof of my house needed repairs. My house is one hundred years old, and my roof was leaking so badly that when it rained it poured inside my laundry room, it looked like a water-fall. I had to set out buckets to catch the water as it rained inside the house.

While the buckets were collecting water inside, I would go on the balcony above the laundry room and vacuum the rainwater that was collected on a tarp. During this process, I would thank God for my house. I thanked Him even though my roof was leaking, while I'm looking at a leaky roof some people have no home. As I cleaned up the water, I would thank Him for my new roof; I would thank Him for my new laundry room.

I did not know when, but I knew God would make a way for me to replace my roof and my laundry room; and He did. Because of the water damage and roof damage, my house was so cold, it literally felt like I was outside. I used space heaters to warm my bedrooms, the kitchen, and the laundry room.

By the grace of God, now my house is nice and warm. June 30th, 2019, Sunday It felt like my mind had been under attack for weeks. I was experiencing emotions that felt like they didn't belong to me, yet, they appeared familiar. I asked God to heal my broken pieces and fix me, because only He could; as I cried out for God to heal me, I saw my phone light up with Mark 5:34 on my Bible app. It read "He said to her, 'Daughter, your faith has healed you. Go in peace and be freed from your suffering."

While in service at the altar, Minister J's message from God to me was to go back to studying God's Word from the beginning. So, I started with my Bible study lessons on my own with week one.

I started with 1 Peter 1:13-16, which reads:

"Be Holy, Therefore, prepare your minds for action; be self-controlled; set your hope fully on the grace to be given you when Jesus Christ is revealed. As obedient children, do not conform to the evil desires you had when you lived in ignorance. But just as he who called you is Holy, so be holy in all you do; for it is written: 'Be holy, because I am holy."

WOW. I did not realize it until now, but how I felt after my husband left, and finding out what he was doing, that anger built up inside of me was what God was warning me about. My thoughts were nowhere near being holy. My God, they were all sinful thoughts.

What sins of revenge are you mentally committing? Give them all to God; only God can release you from your sins and restore you again. Journal your sinful thoughts below.

_____
_____
_____
_____
_____
_____
_____
_____
_____
_____
_____
_____

_____
_____
_____
_____
_____
_____
_____
_____

Now, ask God to forgive you and teach you how to renew your mind so you may forgive your offenders. If you are the offender, go and apologize, and forgive yourself. Record your experiences of how God renews your mind below.

_____
_____
_____
_____
_____
_____
_____
_____
_____
_____
_____
_____

How I Made It Through

*P*rior to the divorce we had a few issues, mostly financial. He would cook, clean the house, do laundry, even iron my work clothes. We played like two kids just playing hide and seek throughout the house. One day I received a message on Facebook from a woman I did not know telling me She and my husband were engaged to be married. And that they had been seeing each other for one year. She said they knew each other and dated in their twenties. I believed the story she told because of the way he was behaving. There were changes such as his phone would ring and he would walk out the room enter another part of the house to answer, that kind of thing. After my husband and I were divorced, I put my best effort into my outward appearance. I got a second job working at a grocery store as a cashier. I would work my first job from 8:00 AM until 4:00 PM, then the second job from 5:00 PM until 10:00 PM.

I started my second job in April 2018. Going to work every day was hard because being in customer service, I had to smile and be courteous. Under normal circumstances that would be easy but having to always smile and be nice while customers told me about their problems and cried on my shoulders was difficult. While I was comforting my customers, I was dying on the inside. However, being at that job helped me to forget my problems for a little while. However, while I was at my day job, my focus had to be on the team I supported. At this job I worked with individuals with disabilities. They were adults but had the mind of children, so I had no time to focus on my problems.

But there were times when I would break down, especially when my team was focused on their activities. I was thankful for my co-workers. They would keep me focused daily because my emotions would get the best of me sometimes. They would either distract me with stories or pray with me. I don't think they ever realized how much I appreciated what they did for me. It is amazing how when helping someone else, you forgot about what you are dealing with, no matter how bad.

Going through this divorce was hard, because I was still coming to terms with everything I had to deal with from my past when publishing my first book.

That book was published in July of 2018, and it took me until December of 2019 to read it without crying. My emotions, feelings of abandonment, and rejection were all still real. So even though I was angry, I was still hoping he would come home. I did not want to feel that sense of abandonment and rejection again. I cried a lot, yelled at God a lot, and asked what else was left for me to endure? Why couldn't I be happy?

I told God that if this was where he wanted me, I would stay there until he released me. I read the Bible every day and that helped give me direction. My emotions were high one day and low the next, but as each day passed, my pain lessened. One day, my daughter Marsha told me to research rejection and abandonment. The article I found listed ten foundations that stem from both rejection and abandonment. As I read the article, I realized I was not crying because my husband left; I was crying because my father had abandoned me all my life.

I met my father for the first time at age twelve, and that was the only time I ever saw him. For most of my adulthood, I was rejected physically, mentally, and emotionally. For most of my childhood, I felt unloved, unwanted, and invisible.

The truth is that sometimes I still felt invisible. I only come alive when I am with my immediate family, children, sisters, and mother. Even when I am in church, after the service is over, I would leave. It's like I didn't know how to interact with others. I simply didn't trust people. I didn't want them in my space, for risk of hurting me. I found myself spending more time talking to God. Sometimes, it feels as if he is right next to me. I asked questions and waited for answers. At times, I got my answers verbally, and sometimes it was through someone else.

One question I asked God after my marriage ended, while crying, was what did I do wrong? Why do people always leave me? His answer was that "sometimes we get involved with people that are broken like us. Dealing with people with the same issues as us shows the other person what they are not ready to deal with in their own life, so they leave to avoid facing their issues".

I found myself thinking back over the eight years I was married, wondering what I could have done differently. At one point I was even blaming myself. This scripture forces me to look at myself and question my part in my marriage ending. 1 Peter 2:1-3 reads, "Therefore, rid yourselves of all malice and all deceit, hypocrisy, envy, and slander of every kind. Like newborn babies, crave pure spiritual milk, so that by it you may grow up in your salvation, now that you have tasted that the Lord is good." I think I did all that I could do but I wonder if I could have done more.

The scripture in 1 Peter 2:4-6 reads, "As you come to him, the living Stone-rejected by humans, but chosen by God and precious to him you also, like living stones, are being built into a spiritual house to be a holy priesthood. Offering spiritual sacrifices acceptable to God through Jesus Christ."

Isaiah 28:16 So this is what the Sovereign Lord says: "See, lay a stone in Zion, a tested stone, a precious cornerstone for a sure foundation; the one who relies on it will never be stricken with panic."

While I worked at the grocery store, I met a customer who I told about my book, and he asked if I was single. I told him I was going through a divorce, and he asked what had happened. I began to tell him what I was going through. He shared his story about his marriage, divorce, and that his wife cheated on him with her co-worker. He said he was devastated, but although he was hurt, he still wanted to save his marriage. He shared that he almost lost everything during the divorce, but for what she got, she would have gotten more if she had just been honest with him. He shared with me how he got over his hurt by traveling, reading, spending time with himself, and lots of self-love.

It is amazing how easy it is for us to see what others' needs are, but it takes heartache for us to take the time to get to know ourselves and really figure out what we need, and what it takes to love ourselves. But, in the end, the customer said that he got back "double for his trouble." Isaiah 41:10 reads, "So do not fear, for I am with you; do not be dismayed, for I am your God. I will strengthen you and help you; I will uphold you with my righteous right hand."

It is important for us to trust God in all that we do, in every aspect of our lives. It is not easy, but we need to be intentional about each day.

After working at the grocery store for ten months, an opportunity presented itself. A friend I worked with, who had worked within the hotel industry for years, accepted a position as a general manager. At a family Thanksgiving dinner, he told me about his new position and asked if I would be his executive housekeeper. I told him I would think about it. I prayed about this decision for over one year as the hotel was being built. During this time, the grocery store had a supervisory position that I thought about applying for, but each time I discussed it with my supervisor, I would get a sick feeling in my spirit. The fact that I would have to leave the morning job that I loved doing, it meant a lot to be a positive influence in the lives of the people I served and supported leaving would break my heart.

Once I told my supervisor that I decided not to apply for the position, that sick feeling I was having went away. Then, in January of 2019, my friend reached out to me and asked what my decision was about the hotel position we talked about. I asked about the salary, and schedule, and decided to take the job. I resigned from both of my current jobs at the same time. In March of 2019, on the last day of my day job, a going away party was given for two employees that were leaving on the same day. However, one of the managers with whom I had a good relationship asked if I would like to stay with the company part-time, in the possible event that I would like to ever come back full-time.

I thought about it and told her "yes". My immediate supervisor signed off on the paperwork and made it official. I would work two days per month, but with all of this, I was still praying and asking the Holy Spirit to guide me on my journey.

I started working my new job at the end of March 2019, assisting in staff hiring, receiving, and setting up the hotel's products, such as guest room supplies, office supplies, and kitchen supplies. However, during orientation, I noticed some things that made me realize that me accepting that job was a test. I believed it was to see if I would revert to the person I was before I started.

For example, prior to me leaving the hotel industry, I did not attend church like I should. I read my Bible, but it was not consistent, and praying was a hit or miss. Don't get me wrong, I loved God, but I was not consistent in building my relationship with the Lord. After I left the hotel industry for the first time in October of 2016, I became an usher at my church, attended Sunday services, Bible studies, and helped in cleaning the church.

This test was to see if I would remain who I became in my walk with God. During orientation the line of communication that was going on was not of God, it was more of chaos. The language that was spoken and the music that was being played during the breaks were not conducive to a professional environment. while I sat and observed I said, "God, you are not the author of confusion, so why am I here? Is this a test?"

As time went on, I would get to work between 8:00 AM and 8:30 AM, and stay until late evening. Sometimes during organizing the hotel, when the hotel was completely set up and the staff training had begun, I felt as though I was just a body for the department because the General Manager would make the decisions. This continued for months. The hotel was finally opened, and the staff was starting to observe what I had already seen for myself. They would come and ask if I was the department manager? They would ask why I didn't make any of the decisions that I told them about. I started feeling in my spirit that it was time to leave because that was not where I belonged.

As I did my one-and-a-half-hour commute every morning and evening, I would talk to God, asking the Holy Spirit questions. One of my questions to God was, "If you sent me here... why? Because my spirit is not settled. If this is a test, I will stay until you decide I'm worthy." In June, I selected a few employees on my team to train for a team lead position, and from those a supervisor would be chosen.

This was weighing so heavily on my spirit that I arrived to work one morning, and my General Manager and I had a conversation. I told him how I felt, and he said he could see that I was not happy, and that even the front office staff was asking what was wrong with me. After that conversation, a girlfriend called me and said, "I was on my way to work on the metro rail. While praying, the Lord showed me you." Without knowing what I was dealing with, she asked, "Do you remember when we worked at the Sheraton"?

I said, "I think so".

"Well", she said, "one morning you were in your office praying while I was in my office praying. You came to me and said something is going to happen. I don't know when and I don't know how. But I feel it in my spirit, and it's coming."

I said, "Yes, I remember that."

She said, "It's time for you to go. That is not where you belong."

That morning right before the phone call, I was sitting in my kitchen praying. The Holy Spirit told me it was time to leave. I went to work and typed my resignation letter. I gave a thirty-day notice. I trained two of the team leaders to take my place. The day I gave my notice, the supervisor from my part-time job called and said, "I need you to cover two shifts for someone who requests time off."

I told him, "Yes, and I need to speak with you about coming back full-time." The hotel job paid more, and I was working with people who I knew working in a profession I loved doing for most of my life, only to get back there and realize I hated that job. It was not for me anymore.

In the other job, I was serving and supporting people with disabilities. That was my passion because while I was away from them, I felt like a part of me was missing. I would call and check on how they were doing and visit them while they were in the community. Although I was struggling to pay my bills, money was not everything. I was happier where I was because what I was doing had meaning and purpose. If I were not in tune with the Holy Spirit, I would have followed my feelings of wanting to make more money to pay bills but be miserable in the process.

My girlfriend's call confirmed what I felt and heard in the spirit. 2nd Corinthians 13:11 reads, "Finally, brothers, rejoice! Strive for restoration, encourage one another, be of one mind, live in peace; and the God of love and peace will be with you."

After I went back full-time to my former job, my spirit, mind, and soul were at peace again. I left the hotel in July of 2019, and by January of 2020, the pandemic started. It started affecting my job in March, but I went to work daily. I was blessed because I was never laid off. I worked more hours because I transitioned into a new position and that department had a staff shortage. Proverbs 3:5-6 reads, "Trust in the Lord with all your heart, and do not lean on your own understanding. In all your ways acknowledge him, and he will make your path straight."

Psalms 37: 4-5 reads "Delight yourself in the Lord, and he will give you the desires of your heart. Commit your way to the Lord; trust in him, and he will act."

I saw no other choice but to trust God with all my heart because I was broken mentally, emotionally, and sometimes, I felt physically broken as well.

I was dealing with rejections from the past compiled on top of new rejections and had to heal.

NOTES: How did you get through your healing process? What keeps you going?

_____

_____

_____

_____

_____

_____

_____

_____

_____

_____

_____

_____

_____

_____

_____

_____

_____

_____

_____

_____

Mental Health

I was on the verge of a nervous breakdown, during the time of my separation leading up to my divorce. I did not feel like myself; It felt like someone else was living in my head. I had no control over my thoughts. All I did was hide under the covers and avoid people. I did not even feel like going to church.

But when I did go, I would sit in the back and cry. I just cried out to God for help. My skin felt like it was crawling; my head felt like bugs were crawling on my scalp. I could not control my thoughts. I was always crying; sometimes, I did not know why.

I had thoughts of suicide, mostly to drive my car into the water when crossing bridges, or to drive into an embankment. This went on for a while, but I knew enough to know that those were not my thoughts. There were times I wanted to just stay in the house in bed, with the covers over my body from head to toe, and I did at times.

Sometimes, I wanted to shut the world out. I even thought about leaving, but then I would think about my babies, my mother, and my sisters. At one point, due to the thoughts of driving my car off the bridge, I started having fears of crossing bridges, and feared that it might happen one day. Even though I never shared my thoughts with anyone, the Holy Spirit did, because I remembered times when ministers and my pastors would pray for me at the altar, and they would specifically pray about the spirit of suicide.

I even remembered that once my Pastor Lamont Jackson prayed, and he mentioned, me wanting to stay in bed and pull the covers over my head. I had that exact feeling a few days prior to him praying over me. Psalms 23 reads,

"The Lord is my shepherd, I shall not want. He makes me lie down in green pastures, he leads me beside quiet waters, he restores my soul. He guides me in paths of righteousness for his name's sake. Even though I walk through the valley of the shadow of death, I will fear no evil, for you are with me; your rod and your staff, they comfort me. You prepare a table before me in the presence of my enemies. You anoint my head with oil; my cup overflows. Surely goodness and mercy will follow me all the days of my life and I will dwell in the house of the Lord forever".

I recite this psalm and say the Lord's prayer often, especially when my spirit feels troubled and I'm not sure why.

NOTE: What do you do when your spirit is troubled, and you're feeling helpless? Record your answers below.

_____

_____

_____

_____

_____

_____

_____

_____

_____

_____

_____

_____

_____

_____

_____

_____

_____

Physical Rejection

I am not sure which is the worst, physical or emotional rejection? Well, I have experienced both, and I am at a place now where I would rather be alone, but God did not design me that way. I am naturally a nurturer, and I enjoy helping others, but now I have asked the Holy Spirit to grant me the spirit of discernment, so I can discern people who carry the spirit of manipulation, and the spirit of jealousy.

People who have been hurt, sometimes enjoy hurting others. Being constantly rejected, whether physically or emotionally, leaves you feeling insecure about yourself, especially if that person rejecting you calls you every name except the one your mother gave you.

While attending school in Jamaica, I had a music teacher who was not very nice. I joined the school choir with my friend, and during rehearsal, as we were singing, she yelled out, "Who is making that sound?

the key is way off base." Naturally, students started looking around, so she had everyone sing to identify the sound she was listening for. It was me. She yelled at me in front of all the other students and told me I should not be singing anywhere. I was devastated and embarrassed. I never sang for anyone to hear me ever again.

John 1:11 reads, "He came to that which was his own, but his own did not receive him." John 15:18 reads, "If the world hates you, keep in mind it hated me first." Psalms 27:10 reads, "Even if my father and mother abandon me, the Lord will hold me close."

Being physically rejected is no reason not to forgive; was it easy? No. But it is possible, forgiving someone for what they have done to us is not so they can feel better about themselves. It is for our healing and salvation.

While we are handing out forgiveness, we should not forget to forgive ourselves. Oftentimes, we forgive everyone that did us wrong but still hold ourselves hostage. Isaiah 53:3 reads, "He was despised and rejected by mankind, a man of suffering, and familiar with pain. Like one from whom people hide their faces he was despised, and we held him in low esteem".

NOTES: Because you were rejected or abandoned, do you think you are a nobody? If so, why.

_____

_____

_____

_____

_____

_____

_____

_____

_____

_____

_____

_____

_____

_____

_____

_____

_____

_____

_____

_____

_____

_____

_____

Emotional Rejection

E motional rejection was something I'd dealt with all my childhood, teenage life, and now as an adult. I didn't know what was worse than having someone around, but emotionally, I was still alone. At least, that's how it felt. I'd felt invisible in the presence of people who were supposed to love and support me. I have dealt with this feeling in both of my marriages. Do you know that feeling where you feel like you were the only one trying to make it work? That's how I felt.

Finally, I gave up, not because that's what I wanted, but I realize that was the only way to save myself. I had also been to church, the place where I should feel accepted, but I felt as though no one saw me.

It was like I was invisible, so the moment church was over, I would rush out the door because standing around watching everyone socializing and having fun while making plans for the day left me feeling rejected. Truth be told, it was not them, it was me because I was emotionally rejected for so long. I no longer trusted people, so I kept my guard up, even when smiling, while in my mind I was thinking, *who are you and what do you want from me?*

I have learned through Bible study lessons at my church, Living by Truth Ministries, ("learning, living and leading" is our motto) that God called us to love everyone, but He did not call us to be in a covenant relationship with everyone. By allowing people access to the innermost personal part of our lives, that is how and when we get hurt.

Matthew 26: 36-38 reads,

Then Jesus went with them to a place called Gethsemane, and he said to his disciples, 'Sit here, while I go over there and pray.' And taking with him Peter and the two sons of Zebedee, he began to be sorrowful and troubled.

Then he said to them, 'My soul is very sorrowful, even to death; remain here, and watch with me.'

Even Jesus had His selected few who He allowed Himself to be in a covenant relationship with.

1 Corinthians 12:9 reads, "My kindness is all you need. My power is strongest when you are weak." So, if Christ

keeps giving me his power, I will gladly brag about how weak I am.

Deuteronomy 14:2 reads, "You have been set apart as holy to the Lord your God, and he has chosen you from all the nations of the earth to be his own special treasure."

Matthew 17:1-4 reads:

"After six days Jesus took with him Peter, James, and John the brother of James, and led them up a high mountain by themselves. There he was transfigured before them. His face shone like the sun, and his clothes became as white as the light. Just then there appeared before them Moses and Elijah, talking with Jesus". Peter said to Jesus, "Lord, it is good for us to be here. If you wish, I will put up three shelters, one for you, one for Moses, and one for Elijah." While he was still speaking, a bright cloud enveloped them, and a voice from the cloud said, "This is my son, whom I love; with Him, I am well pleased. Listen to Him."

Jesus had twelve disciples, but he only chose three as his covenant brothers, even though Jesus had twelve disciples they were not all on the same level in his eyes. We give people privilege they don't deserve and give relationship status that God did not approve.

Sometimes people come into our live they were only supposed to be a friend, or an acquaintance. We turn them into wife or husband and wonder why we have problems later in our marriages.

NOTE: Not everyone is to be in a covenant relationship with us. Who are your covenant partners? Who are your true friends? And why?

_____

_____

_____

_____

_____

_____

_____

_____

_____

_____

_____

_____

_____

_____

_____

_____

_____

_____

Abandonment

*I*t is amazing how our mind can seal bits and pieces of our lives' traumatic experiences away like a time capsule, only to be released when God decides. That was my case, even though I had knowledge of the trauma I experienced as a child. I only had bits and pieces of my memory, after my memories came flooding back like a broken dam. I was in shock because some of the memories were completely new memories. One of these new memories was of being molested as a child by family members, and friends of the family, and having to hear someone I love to tell me to forget about it, because it was in the past. All I wanted was just to gain clarity of what I was remembering to be true.

After building up in my mind who and what I thought my father was, only to one day meet him, and be heartbroken for the first time. Within twenty-four hours of meeting Lester Douglas, I was abandoned by him. He gave me his address and promise that he would always be there for me; but that was a lie, because he never showed up to meet me the next day. I wrote him letter after letter, but there was no answer. Finally, I gave up.

I think my attachment to men came from that moment of me being abandoned and rejected all at the same time. I went through a season in my life where I would only date men who were old enough to be my father but did not know why.

More than twenty years later, the Lord showed me why. I was still looking for that fatherly love. I am now learning that only God can give me what I am looking for; man cannot fill that void or heal me from my broken pieces. Not everyone is to be let into our personal space because then they are given permission to cause harm. I learned that no one could hurt me without my permission.

These are scriptures to show that God is always with us; we only need to trust in Him. Psalms 34:18 reads, "The Lord is near to the brokenhearted and saves the crushed in spirit." Psalms 27: 1-14 reads,

"The Lord is my light and my salvation; whom shall I fear? The Lord is the stronghold of my life of whom shall I be afraid? When evil men advance against me to devour my flesh, when my enemies and my foes attack me, they will stumble and fall.

Though an army besieges me, my heart will not fear; though war breaks out against me, even then will I be confident.

One thing I ask of the Lord, this is what I seek: that I may dwell in the house of the Lord all the days of my life, to gaze upon the beauty of the Lord and to seek him in his temple.

For in the day of trouble he will keep me safe in his dwelling; he will hide me in the shelter of his tabernacle and set me high upon a rock. Then my head will be exalted above the enemies who surround me; at his tabernacle will I sacrifice with shouts of joy; I will sing and make music to the Lord. Hear my voice when I call, O Lord; be merciful to me and answer me. My heart says to you, "Seek his face!" your face, Lord, I will seek.

Do not hide your face from me, do not turn your servant away in anger; you have been my helper. Do not reject me or forsake me, O God my Savior. Though my father and mother forsake me, the Lord will receive me. Teach me your way, O Lord; lead me in a straight path because of my oppressors. Do not turn me over to the desire of my foes, for false witnesses rise up against me, breathing out violence. I am still confident of this; I will see the goodness of the Lord in the land of the living. Wait for the Lord; be strong and take heart and wait for the Lord".

Deuteronomy 31:6 reads, "Be strong and coura-geous. Do not fear or be in dread of them, for it is the Lord your God who goes with you. He will not leave you or forsake you."

Joshua 1:9 reads, "Have I not commanded you? Be strong and courageous. Do not be frightened, and do not be dismayed, for the Lord your God is with you wherever you go."

Isaiah 49:15-16 reads, "Can a mother forget the baby at her breast and have no compassion on the child she has borne? Though she may forget, I will not forget you!"

Think about all the times God was there for you when you didn't even realize it. Maybe he used someone to help turned things around for you or gave you a word of encouragement. Record some of these moments and memories of when God was there for you on the lines below.

Notes

_____

_____

_____

_____

_____

_____

Conclusion

I feel like all my life I have been fighting, struggling, and praying for God's help. From childhood rejection, domestic violence, sexual abuse, and emotional and physical rejection, I can say I have stayed strong not because I wanted to, but because I had to for my children.

Even though my children are grown, they need me as much as I need them.

Looking back and thinking about all the things God has brought me through, I realized I was never alone, even though it felt that way sometimes. The Holy Spirit was always guiding me. I just did not know it and certainly was not in tune.

All my broken pieces will be for my good and God's glory. I only pray that sharing my story will help someone else on their journey through life. My future goal is to help others by one day having a safe place for women and girls who are experiencing domestic violence abuse of any kind, to be able to feel safe while they put themselves on the path to find a successful journey to healing.

It tells us in the scripture of Romans 12:2, "Do not conform to the pattern of this world, but be transformed by the renewing of your mind. Then you will be able to test and approve what God's will is. His good, pleasing and perfect will."

Jeremiah 29:11 reads, "For I know the plans I have for you, declares the Lord, plans to prosper you and not to harm you, plans to give you hope and a future."

Only God can mend our broken pieces. He can put us back together and remove any residue of our brokenness. Mark 11:24-25 reads,

"Therefore I tell you, whatever you ask in prayer, believe that you have received it, and it will be yours. And whenever you stand praying, forgive, If you have anything against anyone. So that your Father also who is in heaven may forgive you your trespasses".

Sometimes it is hard for us to believe that God truly loves us with all our faults, sins, and brokenness. I am here to testify that God loves us unconditionally. Baggage and all. It is us who do not love ourselves.

Once we get to the place where we can forgive our-selves, then we can see God's love for us.

We must learn to keep God first in all that we do. Psalms 34:17-20 reads, "When his people pray for help, he listens and rescues them from their troubles."

"The Lord is there to rescue all who are discouraged and have given up hope. The Lord's people may suffer a lot, but He will always bring them safely through. Not one of their bones will ever be broken".

1 Peter 5:7 reads, "Give all your worries and cares to God, for he cares about you."

Psalms 37:4 reads, "Delight yourself in the Lord, and he will give you the desires of your heart."

Romans 15:13 reads, "I pray that God, who gives hope, will bless you with complete

Happiness and peace because of your faith. And may the power of the Holy Spirit fill you with hope."

I often ask God why I had to go through all that I had been through. I realized that what I endured and *am* going through is so I can be a blessing to someone else

and for God to get the glory out of it. The fact is all that I have been through has been worth it, because it led me to build a stronger relationship with the Father.

Deuteronomy 14:2 reads, "You have been set apart as holy to the Lord your God, and he has chosen you from all the nations of the earth to be his own special treasure."

My plan is to finish school, with my degree in Human Services. Finishing school in 2025 or sooner is my second goal. My first priority is to publish this book. Soon I am going on vacation with my oldest child and her family to Jamaica, and I am looking forward to a great life with Christ at the center of it. Thank you, Jesus.

Are you ready to give God all you have? Write your healing journey conclusion below. Give it to God and watch Him work on your behalf.

Remember, we must forgive ourselves, as well as others. May God bless you and keep you. Only God can mend our broken pieces. I have learned to trust in the Lord with all my heart, and my result is peace of mind. Once you have that, nothing else matters.

NOTES:

_____

_____

_____

_____

_____

_____

"Touches" is the story of my (Marlene J Douglas) journey from abuse as a child and in marriage to graduate high school and become a successful mother. This story is one of Survival. It is also a story of love, the love between a mother and her children.

This book will clear up any confusion you may have. This book gives details about my life from birth and all the emotional, mental, and physical trauma I have endured.

This is a list of numbers of where to seek help:
National Domestic Violence Hotline 1-800-799-7233
TTY 1-800-787-3224
National Sexual Assault Hotline 1-800-656-4673
House of Ruth hotline in Maryland 410-889-7884

The only place I was aware of on this list was the house of Ruth, which assisted me with my first divorce. I will forever be grateful. The other places I was unaware of when I needed help. Hopefully they will be helpful to individuals reading this book. I pray you continue to read the word of God and build your relationship with the Father one verse at a time.

May God bless and keep you!

Thank you to

My children for always being in my corner.

Brandi Brown for telling me stories to keep my mind
occupied during a rough time in my life.

Kara Brummell for praying with me whenever I ask
and did not have the strength to do it alone.

CPSIA information can be obtained
at www.ICGtesting.com
Printed in the USA
LVHW020226080222
710482LV00014B/570